To Luca ♡ Teresa Pelham

Roxy's Forever Home

Roxy

Written by Teresa M. Pelham

Illustrated by Dina Marie Pratt

Roxy's Forever Home

To Doug and the boys, for going along with my crazy ideas.

And to Jan, for your passion and commitment to dogs.

-- TP

To my mother, my guardian angel. Thank you for having faith in me as an artist and encouraging me to follow my dreams. This book is dedicated in your memory.

--DP

O n a hot, sticky
afternoon in
Tennessee, a puppy
with no name sniffed
through a garbage can in
search of something to
eat. Noisy cars whizzed by,
swerving to avoid this little
brown dog with white paws.

MILK Sweet Farm

CHIPS

The puppy with no name didn't know what it felt like to be loved. Nobody had ever held her or told her she was a good dog. She only knew she was hungry. She drank from muddy puddles, not knowing what clean water tasted like. As the summer days got hotter, the little pads on her paws burned against the pavement.

One day, a mom named Melissa and her daughter, Emily, saw the puppy and knew she needed help. They called her to their car and she jumped right in. They drove the puppy to their home and made sure she had plenty of food and water.

The puppy was very skinny and very sick. Melissa and Emily took good care of her until she was all better. Lots of happy dogs lived at their house.

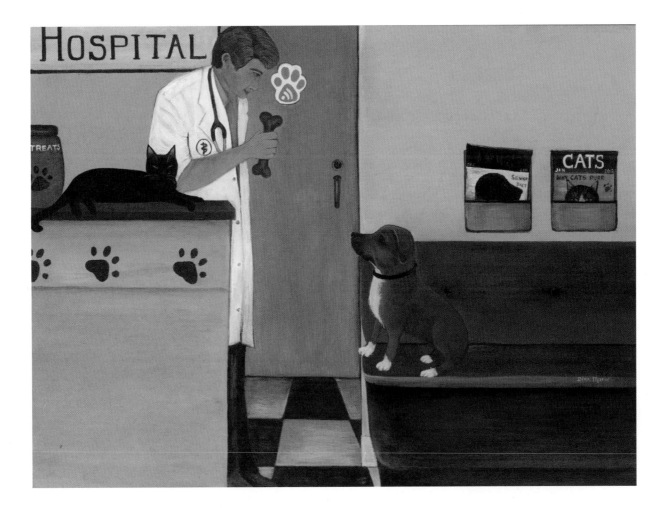

All of the dogs took turns going to see the animal doctor. Sometimes the dogs were scared, but the car rides were fun and all of the people at the doctor's office gave lots of treats and hugs.

arly one morning, Melissa and Emily brought the puppy to a
nice man, who had a big truck filled with lots of other dogs.

"Did you name this one?" the man asked Emily.

"I did!" said Emily. "I named her Roxy."

"Well, hi there, Roxy," the man said.
"We're all going on a road trip."

The puppy thought that Roxy sounded like a good name. And she thought that a road trip sounded good, too. Roxy and the other dogs sniffed each other through their cages. They were all scared and excited. The trip was very long, but Roxy took lots of naps. She dreamed of noisy trucks and muddy puddles and nice people.

Dina Marie

When Roxy woke up, another nice mom named Jan carried her to a car and brought her to a house where kids and dogs and cats all lived together. Chickens and bunnies lived in the big, fun backyard.

"This is your foster
home, Roxy," said Jan.
"But we need to find you
a forever home."

For the next few weeks, Roxy went on lots of great road trips. She sat right on the seat and could look out the window. She went to fields where kids kicked balls into nets, and to a fun store that smelled like dog treats and had cool dog toys. Jan told lots of other people that Roxy needed a home.

A family with three boys visited Roxy all the time. The boys wanted to take her home, but their mom and dad kept saying "No." Roxy wondered if she'd ever find a forever home.

Roxy loved playing with the cats and the big dogs at the foster home. Even though the cats hissed and growled at her, she did not stop trying to make friends with them.

One day, when nobody was looking, Roxy caught one of the chickens. But Jan ran out to the backyard and put an end to all the fun.

T hen one cold, snowy morning, Roxy took a short trip to another house. Jan put her inside a big box with a bow and carried her into the house.

Those three boys who had visited Roxy so many times opened the big box and Roxy jumped out and licked their faces, which tasted like pancakes and bacon. This was their house! The boys' mom and dad were in on the surprise and were so happy to see her. Roxy had found her forever home!

Roxy quickly became a part of the family. She now loves to visit dog parks and chase after big dogs. Her favorite things to chew are number 2 pencils and expensive shoes.

Roxy is very good at learning tricks. She knows how to jump through a hula hoop if a treat is on the other side. She knows how to sit, lie down and roll over.

Dina Marie

And best of all, Roxy knows what
it feels like to be loved.